TIME TO BECOME MYSELF

D0424621

SURPLUS - 1
LIBRARY OF CONGRESS
DUPLICATE

LIBRARY OF CONGRESS
AUG 0 2 1990
COPYRIGHT OFFICE

Southern Christian University Library

AMRIDGE UNIVERSITY
LIBRARY

This book is one in the Prime Time™ series from CompCare Publishers. Prime Time™ books address a wide range of issues and attitudes related to growing older. They are intended primarily, but not exclusively, for people past midlife – especially for those who are choosing to grow older with courage and imagination.

Other books available in
the PRIME TIME™ series:

A Touch of Sage

Never Too Late

Reminiscing Together

TIME TO BECOME MYSELF

Pat Corrick Hinton

Illustrated by Patricia Beaubien

ALABAMA CHRISTIAN
SCHOOL OF RELIGION
LIBRARY

BF
724.85
.S45
H55
1990

CompCare® Publishers

2415 Annapolis Lane
Minneapolis, Minnesota 55441

Control 12593 record 61 disk 19

16726

© 1990 Pat Corrick Hinton
All rights reserved.
Published in the United States
by CompCare Publishers.

Reproduction in whole or part, in any form, including storage in memory
device system, is forbidden without written permission except that portions
may be used in broadcast or printed commentary or review when attributed
fully to author and publication by names.

Library of Congress Cataloging-in-Publication Data
Hinton, Pat Corrick.
    Time to become myself / by Pat Corrick Hinton.
    p.   cm.
    Includes index.
    ISBN 0-89638-222-2
    1. Self-realization in old age. 2. Aging—Psychological aspects.
3. Aged—Psychology. I. Title.
BF724.85.S45H55 1990   90-2044
155.67—dc20   CIP

Cover design by Jeremy Gale
Interior design by Nancy MacLean

Inquiries, orders, and catalog requests should be addressed to
CompCare Publishers
2415 Annapolis Lane
Minneapolis, Minnesota 55441
Call toll free 800/328-3330
(Minnesota residents 612/559-4800)

5   4   3   2   1
94   93   92   91   90

This book is dedicated
to my favorite older persons,
my mother- and father-in-law,
Helen and Howard Hinton

Acknowledgments

Many people helped me make this book a reality. My deepest thanks go to Bob and Virginia Morris for making it all happen; to the members of my classes through the past six years at the Richfield Community Center for Older Adults, especially Marlea, Marge, Mena, Margot, June, Peg, Lonnie, and Amy, who have filled me with ideas and taught me how to try to be fully alive as we age together; to the staff at the Center, especially Lil, Cheryl, Betty, and Susie, who support and encourage me with their foresight and fresh ideas.

Special thanks go to my writing critique group, the Saturday Club: Catharine Brandt, Ceil McLeod, Jane Verby, Vivian Loken, and Claudette Comfort, whose love and support led me to realize I'd rather write than sleep! I thank the Thurston family, for the magic of their lake home; Renee Travis Reilly, the most gifted art instructor I know, for leading me to a whole new way of seeing; and my lifelong

friend, Connie Sandin, who helps me find
humor when there doesn't appear to be any.

Thanks to our young adult children, Laura
and Mark, for unwavering support in spite of a
frequently empty refrigerator, and rooms piled
high with manuscript papers.

Most of all, I thank my husband, Jim, who,
for a quarter of a century, has believed in me,
loved, and inspired me.

Introduction

Making a journey implies change from the starting point until the destination is reached. Writing this book was like going on a journey. At the onset, I believed my goal to be a book of reflections for persons, other persons, over fifty-five. But somehow on the way, the very process of the journey brought subtle changes in me. So that by the end of my book-journey, I'd made the wonderful discovery that I'm truly enjoying this later part of my life-journey. I like being older!

A large part of my enjoyment is due to the older adults who share their lives with me and who constantly deepen and enrich my life and that of others around them. Their ideas and lifestyles are the source for many of these reflections.

What I have learned from the over-fifty crowd—and from my own journey— convinces me of the truth of Carl Jung's statement: "The second half of life is the spiritual work, the questions of meaning." However we have lived our lives up to this point, it now becomes imperative to search daily for deeper meaning. It's time to end the starvation of spirit we may have experienced. And so the search for God as we perceive God to be is the underlying premise of this book.

As this search occupies a prominent place in everyday living, a certain attitude becomes more clear: I have a choice in how I live this part of my journey. As I take the time to clarify my attitude, I find I am constantly becoming more myself. This realization brings satisfaction and even joy to the aging process.

Because we have all been aging since the day we were born, I hope these reflections and quotes speak to every generation. Along with my individual acknowledgments, I especially toast all the warm, wonderful human beings who are choosing to grow older with courage and imagination. The quest is still on!

"Grow old along with me!
The best is yet to be,
The last of life, for which
the first was made.
Our times are in His hand...."
Robert Browning

Invitation

We need to talk about
growing old,
you and I.
Where is age leading us?
What do we hope for?
And fear?
If there ever was a need
for honesty,
now is the time.
Do we trust the
process of the journey?
Are we becoming more ourselves?
Or are we still afraid of change?
How do we view the end?
With dread?
With curiosity?
With longing?

It takes courage to grow old.
Let's make the journey together.

*"One of the wonderful things
about being alive
is that it's never too late."*
Phyllis A. Whitney

Autumn

Growth

Harvest time
is reflection time.

As the farmer gathers
wheat and corn
that grew in summer,
so I gather my thoughts
for a thorough search
of who I am and
where the warmth of summer
led me.

Today I will stand apart
and allow myself the time
to collect,
        to ponder,
                and to glean.

> *"The unreflected life*
> *is not worth living."*
> **Socrates**

Mortality

I am watching maple leaves
change from lush green
to brilliant red and gold,
then die and fall
    to the ground.

I am watching my own body
change from youthfulness
    to age.
I face my own mortality
daily.

In this autumn of my life
can I respond with love
    to rain,
        to sun,
            to frost,
so my colors may be brilliant
to the end?

"The future enters into us, in order to transform itself in us, long before it happens."
Rainer Maria Rilke

Wisdom of Age

There is a wisdom
that comes with age.

The experiences
of my life
are uniquely mine.

I have learned much
that enriches
my daily life.

Today I will
treasure
my inner wisdom.

I will allow it to
grow broader
and deeper.

*"Wisdom
has built herself
a house."*

Proverbs 9:1

Forgiveness

Over and over
I learn the need
to forgive.

Without forgiveness
there can be no
healing.

Forgiveness
allows us to begin
      again.

Who needs my
forgiveness
      today?
Whose forgiveness
do I need?

*"Life
is an adventure
in forgiveness."*
Norman Cousins

Loneliness

To be alone and not lonely
is a gift.
To be lonely and detesting it
is a torment.

If I am lonely,
I can do something to change it.
Difficult as this is,
I can choose
to go out of myself.

I can choose
to find another who is lonely.
I can choose
to find kindred spirits
who can help me
get beyond this.

I can choose.
    God,
        help me.

*"Growth does not cease
to be painful
at any age."*
May Sarton

Insight

The fields have been
harvested.
The ground lies
covered with stubble
or overturned
in huge, black,
rich clumps.

Yet birds find a
feast in what
looks like fallow land.

If the soil of my soul
feels empty
these days,
I will try today to be
open and watchful
for small wonders
and hidden blessings.

Southern Christian University Library
1200 Taylor Rd.
Montgomery, AL. 36117

AMRIDGE UNIVERSITY
LIBRARY

"The real voyage of discovery
consists not in seeking
new landscapes,
but in having new eyes."
Marcel Proust

Time to Rest

The more hectic
my days,
the more I need
to take the time
to rest and
be refreshed.

Is life hectic
because I'm trying
too hard?
It is time
to step aside and
find some balance.

> *"You have to leave room*
> *in life*
> *to dream."*
> *Buffy Sainte-Marie*

Benefits of Aging

Is getting older
as big a problem
as we make it
or have we made it
a problem
because we are afraid
within ourselves
of getting old?

There are many benefits
in the second half of life.
Today, I will concentrate
on those benefits.

> *"Someone has said*
> *of a fine and honorable*
> *old age, that it was*
> *the childhood of*
> *immortality."*
> *Pindar*

Acceptance

The wisdom and number
of my years
instruct me daily
that truth is found
in many opinions
other than my own.

There can be truth
even in what
I consider erroneous.

Do I have enough love
to accept another's
truth?

> *"Become an expert
> in the art of
> discovering the good
> in every person."*
> *Dom Helder Camera*

Fear

Sometimes
I catch myself
building a wall
around who I am.

I can't keep up,
so I fortify
against all possible
invasions and
invitations.

Gentle me, God.
Loosen me up.
What am I afraid of
anyway?

*"You cannot shake hands
with a closed fist."*
Indira Gandhi

Disappointment

Disappointment
can eat away the
marrow of my soul.

I will fight against
its invasion.

Today
I will examine my
expectations
and turn them over
to God.

Today
I begin again.

"To love
means you also trust."
Joan Baez

Enjoy Today

I'd like to risk
being playful today.
    Who says I'm too old
    to be childlike?

It's impossible
for every day
to make sense!
    Today will be fun.

Maybe
this is my chance
to make a dream
come true.

*"My heart is like
a singing bird."*
Christina Rossetti

Risk

The chill I feel in the air
reflects the loss
of loved ones.
An emptiness
leaving me cold
and alone.
    Again.

Do I have it in me
to touch another's
emptiness?
Maybe it's too big a risk
to warm myself
    by reaching out.

        "Love consists in this,
        that two solitudes
        protect and touch
        and greet each other."
            Rainer Maria Rilke

Trust

What do I do
at this stage of life
with the dreams I had
that can't ever come true?

How do I let go
of all that might have been
and never can be?

I turn it over to you, God.
I leave what is broken
and unfulfilled
in your care.

Heal me.

> *"If it were not for hope
> the heart would break."*
> **English proverb**

Acceptance

"It takes so long
to do things."
IT'S THE WAY IT IS.

"My choices
are so limited."
IT'S THE WAY IT IS.

"I don't have much
endurance anymore."
IT'S THE WAY IT IS.

"I'm really younger
than I look."
IT'S THE WAY IT IS.

"And now I have time and peace and
memories and wisdom and perspective!"
IT'S THE WAY IT IS!

*"Faith
is nothing else but
a right understanding
of our being—
trusting
and allowing things to be."*
Julian of Norwich

Spirituality

If I am to grow
in believing and
   in hoping and
      in loving,
I need to surround myself
with like-minded individuals.
I am not in this
alone
unless I choose
to keep myself
isolated.

> *"Empowerment*
> *is the art*
> *of creating life*
> *as you want it."*
> *David Gershan and*
> *Gail Straub*

Giftedness

Instead of complaining
about the sorry
state of the world,
I will find something
to affirm in each person
I meet today.

I will concentrate on
giftedness
and how we can
build up each other.

> *"We can't get rid
> of the craziness
> in the world
> by smashing it."*
> *Joseph Bidwell*

Change

A warm autumn wind
fills me with
nostalgia today.
As leaves float by,
so goes summer and
more relaxed attitudes.
In blows winter soon,
when cold is certain
and relaxation
takes more effort.

The world is changing
all about me but
I am not alone.

With you, God,
I take the next step
toward change.

*"Courage
  is an inner resolution
  to go forward
  despite obstacles."*
              Martin Luther King

Reaching Out

Sometimes I feel
ignored
in this world.

I know
there were times
when I did some
ignoring myself.

Today I will
reach out to another
in friendship.

> *"Since I committed
> myself to others,
> nothing but the
> impossible
> has happened."*
> *R. Buckminster Fuller*

Individuality

In this impersonal world,
I dare to be
personal,
to call my neighbor,
    my child,
        my friend,
            my enemy
    by name.
To call that person
to life today
because I care
that he or she is
in my life.

> *"To be given a name*
> *is an act of intimacy*
> *as powerful*
> *as any act of love."*
> *Madeleine L'Engle*

Becoming Who I Am

One golden leaf
has served its purpose.
Cut off now from
its life-source,
it floats to the ground
to go back to the earth.

I will use this
autumn day
to evaluate who
I have become.

Do I use the
great good gift
of life
within me?

Am I fully human?
Fully alive?

"One of the great lessons
the fall of the leaf teaches,
is this:
Do your work well
and then be ready
to depart when God shall call."
   Tyron Edwards

Possessions

I have lived long enough
to know that accumulating
more does not bring
contentment.
    The more I possess,
    the more I fear to lose.

This day, I choose
to let go of things
I hold too tightly.
I want to be free
    of things.
    I want to be happy.

> *"Teach us to care*
> *and not to care.*
> *Teach us to sit still."*
> T. S. Eliot

Procrastination

At last I have time
to do the things
I've always wanted to do.

Why am I not doing them?

Am I still putting off,
waiting for that
something
to make things happen?

Today I will
make things happen.

Today I will
set my goal and reach it.

> *"Never leave that till*
> *tomorrow which*
> *you can do today."*
> *Benjamin Franklin*

Losses

Mr. Kretchmer's old drug store
has been turned into a high-rise.
It's downright depressing!
I've lost Friends
    Loved ones,
        Neighbors, and
            Co-workers.
I'm losing my Sight,
    Hearing,
        Energy,
            Memory,
Looks,
    Income,
        House,
            and Dreams.

God, help me!
Now that I've listed all these losses,
I see that I have
less to worry about!

*"A cheerful heart is a good
medicine,
but a downcast spirit dries up
the bones."*
                    Proverbs 17:22

Enjoying Today

I seem to be slowing down.

Today, rather than
complain,
I choose to count
this slower pace
as blessing.

How often in my younger days
did I rush past
opportunities
to appreciate
the now,
    the present,
        the gift of being?

> *"Try to be happy*
> *in this very present moment."*
> *Thomas Fuller*

Letting Go

Autumn is a time
of letting go.

If I am grieving
or feeling loss
of any kind,
may I accept these
as part of my own
transformation.

May I allow
the healing to begin.

> *"As in the physical world,*
>   *so in the spiritual world,*
>   *pain does not*
>   *'last forever.' "*
>   *Katherine Mansfield*

Choices

In this season of change,
I sense
separation
from the familiar.

Decisions are waiting.
Choices need to be made.

What shall I gather
in my harvest?
What should I discard?

Are my choices
leading me to
a deeper quality of life?

Is time my friend?

*"Life must be understood
backwards.
But it must be lived
forward."*
    Soren Kierkegaard

Death's Mystery

I don't want to
brood about death,
but I want to
face directly
what it means.

What a great mystery
it is to know for a fact
that someday
I will not be here
in this body.

And who and where
will I be?

After all this work
to become who I am,
I trust death
is simply a door
to a new reality.

*"Every ending
is a new beginning."*
    Author unknown

Gratitude

The journey
of my life is a
journey to truth.

Each step along the way
is meant to lead me
to new realizations,
        greater insights,
                deeper love.

In this harvest time
may I reap my crops
with joy,
grateful for growth,
confident
that I am loved
by my Creator
        without condition.

*"Earth's crammed with Heaven
and every common
bush afire with God."*
Elizabeth Barrett Browning

Judgments of Youth

Have we taught our young ones
to be so judgmental
about the choices we make?
Or are they getting even?

How can we help them
understand
that we need their support,
that we don't need
to be told that we are
all wrong or all right
or even remarkable.

What we need to hear
is that we are loved.

"But the God-given need for love
is ageless and essential,
and something for which we
may be proud to fight."
Marion Pease Davis

Feelings

Many of us
were brought up
to "be nice."
That's not all bad,
but that approach
buried alive
many of my feelings.

I will take
some time today
to be in touch
with how I really feel.

> *"To feel
> what one feels
> instead of what
> one ought."*
> *Virginia Satir*

Defining Death

Why are we afraid to die?
Is it because death is such
an unknown?
Is it because we think
it may be the end of everything
    after all?

God, help me face
my own dying.
Help me define what it is,
accept it,
and trust you to be with me
    on my journey.

> *"It is ourselves*
> *and not outward circumstances*
> *who make death*
> *what it can be,*
> *a death freely and*
> *voluntarily accepted."*
>   *Dietrich Bonhoeffer*

The Wisdom of Age

When I am hurt
or offended by another,
especially someone
close to me,
may I not offend in return
but reflect long enough
to use the wisdom
of my years.

May I respond
with grace that will be
life-giving
to each of us.

"If only I may grow
firmer, simpler,
quieter, warmer."
Dag Hammarskjold

Memories

Would anyone believe
the stories of my youth?

Would anyone care?

My memories are filled
with the things and people
I loved when I was young.

I am
surviving
through those memories.

Is today the day
to share
my younger self?

Who will listen?

> *"We must always have
> old memories and
> young hopes."*
> *Arsene Houssaye*

New Skills

Whatever my age
I'm not too old
to develop some skills.
Do I have talents
that I've ignored
thinking it's too late
to help them grow?

What did I set aside
years ago
that could enrich
my life now?

I'm still in charge
        of me.

*"Whatever you are
from nature,
keep to it;
never desert your own
line of talent."*
        Sydney Smith

Busyness

Busyness is robbing us
of thoughtfulness.

This modern world
is so intent on
accomplishment
of private goals,
there's no time or energy left
for caring for each other.

"I've been so busy,"
is today's alibi.
Where will all this lead us?

Slow us down, Lord,
before we rush off
the face of the earth.

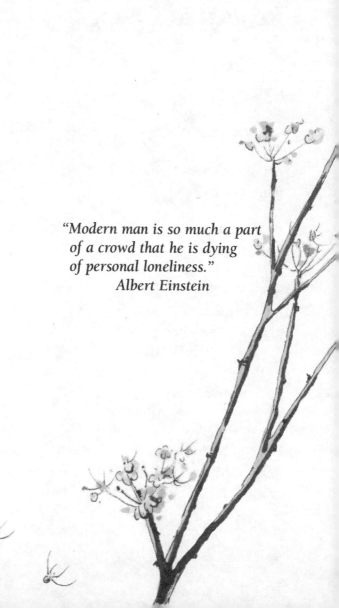

"*Modern man is so much a part of a crowd that he is dying of personal loneliness.*"
Albert Einstein

Refusal to Change

Long, gray days
are getting me down.
The sameness of gray,
day after day,
reminds me of my own
refusal to change.

I am stuck in my
fear of failure,
deluding myself
by denying
my own will
to make new choices.

At this moment, God,
I acknowledge my
weakness.
By your power
create in me
fresh hope.

*"There is pain in staying
the same, and there's pain
in change. Pick the one
that moves you forward."*
Earnie Larsen

Priorities

What happened to time
when I turned fifty?
It seems to be on fast-forward,
and the future
is suddenly shortened.

I've spent half a century and more
learning how to do things
and now I wonder if I will
have time to accomplish
all that I've been waiting
to have the time to do!

It's plain I won't have time
to do it all.

Today, I promise myself
to do what is important to me
        and to relish it
                as thoroughly as possible.

*"To effect the quality of a day
is the highest of arts."*
Henry David Thoreau

Gratitude

There are nights
when sleep just won't come.
In those moments and hours,
it's easy for worry to slip in.

Next time I'll be ready.

Instead of worry
I'll name each gift
that comes to me
through my senses:
      Eyes—Golden trees and children playing
      Nose—Burning leaves and bracing air
      Ears—Birds singing and rain falling
      Touch—Loving pet and handmade quilts
      Taste—Good desserts and neighborly tea.

Gratitude leaves no room
for worry.

*"Gratitude is the memory
of the heart."*
H. V. Prochnow

The Process of Life

The elm tree
outside my window
stands as a symbol
of my life.
Some leaves are green,
still full of vigor.
Others are in the
process of change.

The dark, bare branches
speak loudest.

Today
I accept the
process
of my years.
I am
trusting and hopeful
toward all that is
yet to come.

*"Life is a school of love...
made up of successive stages."*
Paul Tournier

Surviving, with Love

I don't move about
as easily as I used to,
but I have learned
one thing:
to survive
I must be in touch
with living, breathing
persons.
>   Not surrounded
>   every moment
>   but often enough
>   to love and be loved.

>   *"To live in love*
>   *is life's*
>   *greatest challenge."*
>   *Leo Buscaglia*

The Isolation of Age

Too often,
younger, faster-moving people
isolate me.
Worse yet,
they even ignore me.

I want to say to them:
"Slow down, honey.
You'll soon be
where I am,
and you'll be here
before you know it!"

> *"Just because the message*
> *may never be received*
> *does not mean*
> *it is not worth sending."*
> *Segaki*

Bridges

Some persons my age
seem determined
to find the differences
between generations.
Searching out differences
creates unhappiness.

Isn't it time
we actively listen
to each other?
Isn't it time
we build bridges
of confidence?

"It is the understanding
that sees and hears;
it is the understanding
that improves everything."
Epicharmus

Celebrating Health

Every day that I can
laugh and
    sing and
        talk and
move
I know I am far richer
than if I owned
a million material
things
which often limit
my gifts to
laugh and
    sing and
        talk and
move!

> *"The first wealth*
> *is health."*
> **Ralph Waldo Emerson**

Winter

The Wonder of Life

I am growing older
and someday I'll be old.
I will strive to keep
my working parts healthy.

I accept my diminishing
strength and memory
as part of
the miracle of life.

*"Find wonder
in all things."*
Author unknown

Living Today

The weather is on the verge
of change
and so am I.
Remnants of fall color
still cling to trees and bushes.
One day is warm,
the next cold.

It's time
to let go of all
that has been
done and said.
It's time
to live today well.

Today is all I have.

*"For everything there is
a season....
A time to seek
    and a time to lose;
a time to keep,
    and a time to cast away."*
    Ecclesiastes 3:1,6

Gratitude

When I hear music
today
I will remember
with love and thanks
to name all the
people and things,
places and laughter
that bring
harmony
into my life.

*"There is no music
in a rest,
but there is the
making of music..."*
John Ruskin

Respect for My Body

On these days
when my body protests
moving from here to there,
I want to listen
to my creaks and groans
and allow them gently
to rest.

May the loving respect
I give my body
spill into my soul
as joy.

> *"Laziness
> is love's opposite."*
> **M. Scott Peck, M.D.**

Friendship

I have a friend
of many years
who appears to have
forgotten me.

It's hard to not feel
needed anymore.

I know my friend
is very busy.
Her health is better
than mine and she has more
money to spend than I do.

Should that make a difference?

I don't want to lose her friendship.

Can I risk reaching out to her
one more time?

*"To have a friend
takes time."*
Georgia O'Keefe

A Greater Power

By now, I should know that
I can't go on, day after day,
ignoring my spiritual side.
If I am to make any sense
of good things,
    bad things,
        problems,
            and setbacks,
to say nothing of success,
I need to acknowledge that
a Power greater than myself
is working for my good and
the good of all creation.

*"God is at work
in the heart of the world."*
Karl Rahner

The Meaning of Time

In my working days
I never dreamed
how the meaning of time
would change in retirement.
Structured time
was more valuable
than I thought.

Without specific work
to go to, I now have to
make a special effort
to have something of value
in each day.

Light my way, God.

> *"I am an artist at living,*
> *and my work of art*
> *is my life."*
> **Suzuki**

Busyness

Isn't it time I stop
inventing things
to fill the spaces
of my days?
Little gods of
busyness,
of constant activity,
of filling every
moment
with something to
occupy my restless thinking.

Isn't it time
I learn how
to simply
be?

"O senseless man
who cannot make
a worm,
and yet makes gods by dozens."
Michel E. de Montaigne

Young Inside

When I was young
I viewed middle age
as old.

Now that I'm in
middle age or beyond,
I feel I've lived
a long life
which is going by
too quickly.

I'm still young
inside.
I only look older.

> *"Old age isn't so bad*
> *when you consider the*
> *alternative."*
> *Maurice Chevalier*

Blessings

Winter is upon us.
In the past, I've often
allowed this to get me down.

This year, I choose
to count the good things
that come with colder weather.

Even if it takes
all winter
I will count my blessings!

*"Only with winter-patience can we bring
the deep-desired, long-awaited spring."*
Anne Morrow Lindbergh

The Future

The future takes on
a different meaning now.
I know my own is limited.

Younger people are
taking over the world,
doing good things,
making improvements.
Making changes.

There is a sadness and confusion
in this, as if my departure
from this world
is beginning prematurely.

Slowly, I am being replaced.
It's the natural order of things.

God, guide us all.

*"Now that I am old there are times
when I feel I am barely here,
no room for me at all."*
    Florida Scott-Maxwell

Aging

I am aware
that I am not as alert
as I used to be.
I can let this fact
upset and discourage me,
or I can
be thankful
for all the
parts of me
that work.

> *"Gratitude
> is a soil on which
> joy thrives."*
> *Berthold Auerbach*

Mending

Parts of me are
wounded,
scattered, and hurt.
I truly want to mend.
I want to be a whole
and healthy person.

I choose today
to allow God
to heal and
cleanse me.
I am not afraid.
God is with me.

"Life breaks us all
sometimes,
but some grow strong
at broken places."
Ernest Hemingway

Compassion

Today
I will not allow
my own troubles
to close me off
    from others.

Today
I will watch
with an open heart
for ways to be
present
    to another.

There is always
someone
whose needs are greater
    than my own.

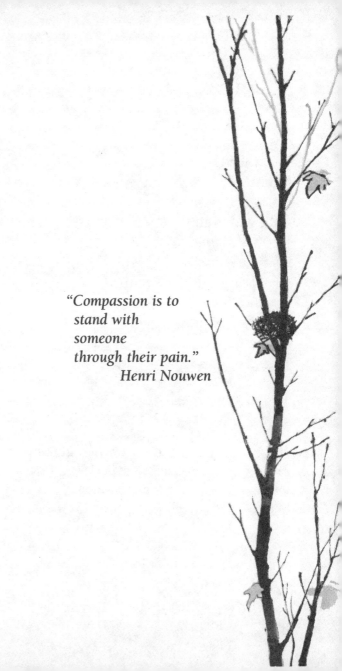

"Compassion is to stand with someone through their pain."
Henri Nouwen

Choices

All of life is
darkness and light.
Today I choose the
light within me
    to brighten the
    dark places of
    pain or disappointment
    or illness.
Doubts and uncertainty
need not be
negative.

I choose life!

> *"The most beautiful thing
> we can experience
> is the mysterious."*
> **Albert Einstein**

Forgiveness

Long years of living
have taught me that
mutual forgiveness
isn't always possible.

I am responsible for being
a forgiving person myself
but I cannot control
how or if another person
forgives me.

God, I trust in you
to heal what I cannot.

> *"We must be saved by the final
> form of love
> which is forgiveness."*
> *Reinhold Niebuhr*

Comfort of Age

There's a certain comfort
in being part of this age group.
We seem to understand each other.

We aren't afraid to risk
a smile or small talk.

We know we don't have to
impress each other or
conform to another's standards.

We share experience, memories,
and wisdom—
and we're still growing!

> *"Reverence*
> *is one of the signs*
> *of strength."*
> *Author unknown*

Positive Thoughts

We can control
what we allow ourselves
to think.

I will take great care
today
to feed my mind
affirming,
positive thoughts.

Healthy actions
are sure
to follow.

> *"Negative opinions*
> *of yourself*
> *block out*
> *your own reality."*
> *John Catoir*

Experience as Teacher

Today
I am going to give thanks
for what experience
has taught me:
    that I can choose
    how to respond to
    what life brings to me;
        that I can work through
        grieving and loss and
        grow through these realities;
that I can find rainbows
after every storm;
        and that I can't change others,
        only myself.

God, I thank you for the freedom
experience brings.

"Each of us has the power to decide whether or not our own aging is a positive venture."
Dave Kachel

Things to Share

The accumulation
of things
throughout my life
is getting in the way.

It's time to peel away
these hindrances—
not to accumulate more.

I've put this off
long enough.

Who needs what I
have to share?

> *"When we die we carry*
> *in our clutched hand*
> *only what we have*
> *given away."*
>   *Peter Maurin*

Yearnings for Spring

God, are you here?
The cold
comes creeping in.
The days are short.
The nights are long.
I yearn for light,
    for air,
        for gentle weather.

Be here
    in my hunger,
        in my longing.
Help me.

> *"Love winter
> when the plant
> says nothing."*
> **Thomas Merton**

A Time to Rejoice

I am committed
to getting the most out of life.
I will not age
according to the rules.

I don't feel old,
so why do what old people do?

I take care of myself and
dress the best I can.
I'm a lot more casual and
relaxed and probably
better-looking
than I was ten years ago.

And I work when I choose.

Why isn't everyone anxious
to be where I am?

    Hallelujah!

*"Man's mind, stretched
to a new idea, never
goes back to its
original dimensions."*
        Oliver Wendell Holmes

Young Listeners

I'd like to tell
the younger generation
how comforting they are
when they listen to my story.

As I grow older,
society and endangered health
threaten my feelings of
self-worth.

Some days I have to work hard
to know who I am.

So, when willing ears
appreciate how I have
lived my life,
my spirit soars and
I feel truly worthwhile.

*"We are one, after all, you and I;
together we suffer, together exist,
and forever will recreate each
other."*
        Teilhard de Chardin

Honesty

If the air outside is
crisp and clean or
heavy and dull,
today I will try
to clear the air
inside my home.

I will face,
directly and honestly,
my feelings,
my needs,
and my connectedness
to others.

> *"We must muster
> the insight and the courage
> to leave folly and
> face reality."*
> *Albert Schweitzer*

Cheerfulness

When I get down,
I tend to drag others
down with me.

When I'm optimistic
and cheerful,
that spreads too.

This day I choose
to brighten the journey
of those around me.

*"A good laugh
is sunshine
in a house."*
William Makepeace Thackeray

Mortality

Winter puts me face to face
with my own
mortality.
I am living a mystery,
wondering when and how
    it will happen.

When my time comes,
I hope for the gifts of
a clear mind and
the presence of a friend
or loved one
who will help me keep
my spirit vital
    to the end.

> *"It is as natural to die*
> *as to be born."*
> *Francis Bacon*

Creativity

I am a human being.
Therefore, I am
creative.
I can solve problems,
or I can solve problems
creatively.

This day I will silence
my inner critic.
I will open myself
to the wisdom and
imagination
I know are within me.

> *"Creativity is strong
> only
> if critical thinking
> is weak."*
> *Peter Elbow*

Loneliness

If I listed all the things
I fear about aging,
loneliness would be at the top
or near it.

With each birthday
I see my circle of loved ones
diminish.

I can allow these losses
to diminish me
or I can refuse
to permit my aloneness
to take over.

I can use whatever is
working in me
to remedy my own situation.

*"Wisdom is ofttimes nearer
when we stoop
than when we soar."*
William Wordsworth

Choosing Love

I carry within me
the potential
to be a loving person.

How will I choose
to live today?
    Serving only myself
    and my own needs?
    Or open and ready
    to share who I am
and who I can become?

What would love do today?

> *"In the evening*
> *of this life*
> *we will be judged*
> *on love."*
>
>   *Catherine of Siena*

Reaching Out

When we have sunk low,
is there a greater
challenge
in daily living
than to urge oneself
to touch the pain
of another?

And is there a
greater
message of love
than to realize that,
by our reaching out,
we ourselves are
healed?

> *"To ease
> another's heartache
> is to forget
> one's own."*
> **Abraham Lincoln**

An Open Heart

Some days
I am too tired
to move about much.
If I am physically
confined
to a small space,
may I not close in
upon myself,
but keep my heart
wide open
to every message
of love
that comes my way.

May I not
miss a chance
to love another.

*"The refusal to love
is the only
unbearable thing."*
    Madeleine L'Engle

Inner Quiet

The cold outside
invites me to
keep warm inside.

Perhaps this is a day
for inner quiet,
a chance to get
in touch with me,
and what's going on
inside me.

Today
    I will be
        my friend.

> *"It is tranquil people*
> *who accomplish much."*
> *Henry David Thoreau*

Accepting Death

The stillness of the earth,
the cold ground and
bare, black branches
remind me that I need
to come to terms
with death.

If I have not yet
accepted my own death,
I cannot live life
fully.
What do I fear?
How can I transform
this fear?

> *"Fear is the mind-killer.*
> *Unacknowledged fear*
> *is the worst kind of fear."*
> *Frank Herbert*

Liking Where I Am

I like this age.

I revere the wisdom
only experience
can impart.
On better days
I even take things
in stride.
My expectations
are more realistic.

I like this age.
I'm just surprised
I got here so quickly.

*"The tragedy of
old age
is not that one is old
but that one is young."*
Oscar Wilde

Loneliness

I think my own loved ones
do not intend to
desert me.
But there are times
when I feel
isolated and forgotten.

I know their lives are busy,
but I wish I could explain
how long my days can be,
how difficult it is to be
sick and alone,
or how exhausting it is
to have to make
decisions by myself.

God, help me
to help them understand.
I'm glad *you're* here!

"Cast me not off in my old age;
as my strength fails, forsake me
not."

Psalm 71:9

Choosing Life

There is still a
little insidious pull

inside me
that resists change.

Am I afraid
to risk failure?

Am I afraid
of making my own dreams
come true?

God,
deliver me from
self-delusion.

Let me choose life!

*"When you're through
changing,
you're through."*
       Bruce Barton

Suffering

I would just as soon
do without affliction and pain,
but this doesn't seem to be
the choice.

Suffering is often
pervasive
either within me or
in those I love.

We are not in this alone.
We have each other and
we have a Creator
who will help us.

God, and loved ones,
hear my cry:
"Help!"

*"The way past the pain is to
go all the way through it."*
Alla Renée Bozarth

The Gift of Aloneness

Being alone
can be a great teacher.

Whether I am alone
by choice or from
loss of a loved one,
my solitary world
can teach me peace,
and an appreciation
of the inner stirrings
of my soul.

May I not resist these
quiet moments
but let them lead me
to greater giving
of the self I discover.

*"In solitude we discover
our life is not a
possession to be defended
but a gift to be shared."*
Henri Nouwen

Recording Memories

I have loved so many
people, places, things
throughout my life.
I need to
pass these loves on
to those who come after me.

Today, I will
begin my story
on paper,
    onto a tape,
        or tell it to another
        to record.

*"We have a need
to say we were here."*
Patricia Hampl

Peace of Heart

The search for peace
is an ongoing process.
Some think
it's a place you try
to get to.
My experience says
it has to start
right here, within me.

I won't ever find peace
"out there"
unless I find it first
within my own heart.

> *"If you give yourself*
> *to the cause of peace*
> *you will find great joy."*
> *Dr. Helen Caldicott*

The Meaning of Today

I've decided,
Quality
must take over
Quantity.
Searching for
depth and meaning
in each day
becomes a priceless
challenge.
The number of my years
is secondary
to drawing meaning
out of daily living.

I choose to grow
in what is internal and
eternal.
I choose life!

*"It is the quality of life
that counts and not the
number of years we live."*
            Elizabeth Kubler-Ross

Grandchildren

Winter is a pensive time.
Memories and longings
well up and converge.
I was young
such a short time ago.
What will happen to all
I worked for and enjoyed?

Who will my grandchildren
grow up to be?
Will the air they breathe be cleaner?
Will they live on distant planets?

Will they, at last, be free from
having to fight in wars?

God, I can only trust that
you will care for them
as you have cared for me.

*"Relying on God has to begin
all over again every day
as if nothing yet had been done."*
C. S. Lewis

Simplicity

My ability to
complicate things
is amazing.

Today I ask for help
from God
to approach the
problems of my day
with simplicity and
with a clarity
that will bring
success and progress,
wholeness and health.

"In character,
in manners,
in style,
in all things,
the supreme excellence
is simplicity."
    Henry Wadsworth Longfellow

Reverence for Creation

Nothing renews the spirit
    like a fresh snowfall
    in the early morning.

Snow piles on black branches
    that hold the promise of spring.

Mounds of white crystals
    sparkle as the sun rises.
Each flake a fantasy.
Texture, crisp air, LIFE,
    in all this simple beauty.

God, help us to care for
    this magnificent earth.
Teach us reverence
    for everything you have created.
And thanks.

"Teach your children what we have taught our children, that the earth is our mother...love it as we have loved it."
Chief Seattle of the Suquamish Nation

Hope

Just when winter is dragging on,
a crimson red cardinal
perches on a snow-covered pine branch
outside my window.
He looks intently,
searching for food.
Nourishment is hard to find.

But I know and he knows that
beneath the snow
the green of the tree
promises feasts to come.

He begins his nesting song
and I am filled with hope.

Not even winter lasts forever.

*"Beneath the winter's snow
lie germs of summer flowers."*
John Greenleaf Whittier

Spring

Nurturing

New growth
stretching up through
black earth
invites me to ask
where I am going
in this fresh, new world
    of springtime.

What needs to be planted
on the path I have chosen?
What needs nurturing
and loving care
    in me
        and in those I love?

> *"The most vital right*
> *is the right*
> *to love and be loved."*
> *Emma Goldman*

Becoming Myself

As my wisdom grows and
experience deepens,
I guard against the
fatal habit
of thinking I must
say something
on every subject and
on every occasion.

I am not expert
yet.
I am still
in process.

> *"What I am to be
> I am now becoming."*
> **Author unknown**

Living Today

Today, what really matters
is what I live and feel,
    just for today.

Whether I am full
of limitations
or wise beyond expectations,
this is who I am
    today.

Whatever else I might be,
I pray to be
    authentic.

> *"To know*
> *That which before us lies*
> *in daily life*
> *Is the prime wisdom."*
> *John Milton*

A Generous Spirit

When I find myself
saying "I can't"
because of my
physical limitations,
I pray now
to remember that
whatever my body
can't do,
my heart,
    my mind,
        and my will
can remain faithful
to a generous spirit,
    to understanding,
        and to love.

> *"Fidelity*
> *is the fairest flower*
> *of love."*
>   *Columba Marmion*

The Meaning of Life

What do I have to do
    to make more sense
    out of living and dying?
I try to live my life
    with dignity and meaning.
Yet, the questions
constantly recur—
    "Why are we here?"
    "Is this all there is?"

Perhaps this is the day
in which I need to
concentrate my energy on
    my own spiritual cry.

> *"Spirituality—*
>   *the foundation from which*
>   *you answer the questions*
>   *that matter."*
>   **Earnie Larsen**

Interests and Eternity

My interests
take me many places
    to do many things.

Do my interests
distract me
    from my real needs?

Or do my interests
integrate
my needs with
my growing toward
    what is
        eternal
            within me?

"The best way
to know God
is to love
many things."
Vincent Van Gogh

Fear

Fear is a nuisance!

It gets in my way
and tells me I am
incapable.

This day
I will keep fear
in its proper place:
inactive.

I am gifted.
I am alive
and ready to be
the best I can be.

Today I am
empowered
to be authentic and
unafraid.

*"To fear a thing is to
give it power over you."*
      Moorish proverb

Busyness

Did someone say
getting on in life
means filling
every minute with
busyness?
I thought I was
beyond that!

Slow me down, Lord.
Too much rushing
brings anxiety.

I want to savor the
NOW.
Today.
    Here.
        This minute.

*"When you get older
it takes a lot longer
to do nothing."*
	Catharine Brandt

Transformation

As the seasons change
I find my own rhythm.
In the fresh air of these spring days,
I want to respond
with an open heart
to the transforming
sights and sounds,
textures and tastes
of our world made new,
     again.

> *"Airs, vernal airs, breathing*
> *the smell of fields and grove,*
> *attune the*
> *trembling leaves."*
> *John Milton*

Sorrow

I carry the sorrows
of my years
    within me.
Often, not even loved ones
    know.

Some burdens
have gotten lighter
    with time.
Others
weigh heavier still.

I give my secret pain
to you, God.
    Help me!

> *"Earth has no sorrow*
> *that Heaven cannot heal."*
> *Thomas Moore*

Laughter

God, help me laugh
when I can't remember
where I left my shoes,
    or my glasses,
    or my wallet.

Help me laugh
when my mind goes blank
and leaves me in
mid-sentence.

Don't let me take myself
too seriously,
    or anyone else,
    for that matter.

Loosen me up, God.
Loosen us all from
our serious expectations.
Teach us all to say,
    "So what?"

*"The day most wholly lost is
the one on which one does not
laugh."*
Nicolas Chamfort

Gratitude

Each day is a gift.
Today I want to pay
special attention
to all the good
that constantly comes
    my way.

I will be alert
to the blessings
    of the moment.

I will keep
annoyances
    in their place
and open my arms wide
with thanks
    for the gift of life.

*"The afternoon of life
must also have a
significance of its own
and cannot be merely
a pitiful appendage
to life's morning."*
Carl Jung

Pain

My good health
is a great gift.

But when pain
threatens to
take over,
whatever its source,
I can choose
to cling to it and
be paralyzed by it.

Or I can name it
and choose to move forward,
to grow because of
its very existence.

> *"Pain is a very
> human way
> of demanding
> change."*
> *Leo Buscaglia*

Resilience

My generation
has witnessed more
wars, inventions, and
reversals of values
than any other.
We feel we have adjusted remarkably.

God, I thank you
for the courage and
resilience with which
you have gifted
my generation.

Give vision and strength
to all who come after us.

> *"Life, like love, cannot thrive*
> *inside its own threshold*
> *but is renewed as it offers itself.*
> *Life grows as it is spent."*
> *Ardis Whitman*

Spirituality

Sometimes I feel
so connected
to the Universe,
so much a part
of all that is.

Today I will
take the time to
let go of the
materialistic
in my life and allow
my spiritual,
inner self
to become visible.

> *"The longest, hardest*
> *journey*
> *is to our inmost spaces."*
> *Dag Hammarskjold*

Seeds of Hope

Spring is planting time,
    a time of growth and
    transformation.

This day,
I will take great care
to plant healthy
thoughts and ideas
    in my mind and heart.

I will plant seeds of hope
    that will lead me
        to productive actions.

> *"There is no time like Spring,*
> *When life's alive in*
> *everything...."*
>   *Christina Rossetti*

Individuality

How easy it is
to stereotype.
We hand out names
of young,
middle-aged,
and old
and forget we are
talking about
people.

I don't like
being stereotyped,
so today I will
think of others
and myself
as the
individuals
we are.

*"Let us reflect
that each one of us
is a thought of God."*
        Mme. Swetchine

Loss of Opportunity

Gray gloom outside
is settling inside
my soul.
I feel heavy
with unshed tears,
mourning the loss of
opportunities I missed or
    didn't try or
        failed to complete.
I am face to face
with the tears of things.

Are you here, God?
I need to know
you are present,
even in my
unfinished potential.

*"Life only demands from you
the strength you possess.
Only one feat is possible—
not to have run away."*
     Dag Hammarskjold

Gratitude

I have been blessed
with many gifts
of mind,
     heart,
         and spirit.

With gratitude
I will count my blessings
and search for one
new way
to share who I am.

> *"The great moments*
> *of life are*
> *faith, hope, love,*
> *and insight."*
> *Carl Jung*

A Look Inside

There are days when
I look in the mirror
and all I see are wrinkles!

I wish that were
my only sign
of aging!

But then,
wrinkles are only
skin deep.

It's time to have
a look inside
for signs of spring.

> *"Have a care*
> *lest the wrinkles*
> *in the face*
> *extend to the heart."*
> *Marguerite de Valois*

Pain

When heartaches and
body pain
threaten to take over,
it would be easy
to quit.

But I'm not in this
alone.
I am created,
sustained,
and loved
by a Creator
who loves me
and accepts me
as I am—
      warts and aches and all.

*"The purpose of life...
is to live it...
to reach out eagerly
and without fear."*
        Eleanor Roosevelt

Reaching Out

More often than I
care to admit,
there's a temptation
to think I have
done enough, so now
I'll just take care of me.

God, deliver me from
turning my back.

Strengthen me to try always
to reach out to the helpless
and those who have no voice.

Help me to use my gifts,
great or small,
to fill even one person's need
to be cared about today.

"The greatest suffering
is being lonely,
being unwanted,
being unloved,
just having no one."
        Mother Teresa

Living Today

I'll take today as it comes.
I might make plans for tomorrow,
    but I refuse to worry about it.

Today is for me,
a gift,
an opportunity,
a day to find
my own current of life,
my own ability
to laugh and to feel,
to think and to love.

I'll take today as it comes
    and I'll be grateful for it.

*"We must always change,
renew, rejuvenate ourselves;
otherwise we harden."*
Goethe

Dignity in Differences

If I want to be a
truly loving person,
there can be no room
for judgment of others.

Love urges me
to respect the dignity
of every person,
no matter what they have
or lack,
no matter how
different they are
from me
       or how alike.

> *"The more one judges,*
> *the less one loves."*
>   *Honore de Balzac*

A Need for Listeners

Do friends remember me?
Do people know I'm here?
I have so much to tell
but who's around to hear?
Words rise up in me
waiting to be pronounced,
announced,
and who will listen?
Who cares to hear
what I have to say?

I am all questions.
Who will help me find answers?

Who loves me enough to listen?

"Pain is pain and
sorrow is sorrow.
It hurts. It limits.
It impoverishes. It isolates....
But the gifts God can give with it
are the richest the human spirit
can know."
                    Margaret Clarkson

Patience

How is it
the younger generation,
    even my own offspring,
sometimes try to
convert me
to their young ideas
    as if only they
    are right
        and I am old and foolish?

One among us
has to be mature enough
to endure with patience
    and it had better
        be me.

And don't call me old.

> *"It takes one a long time*
> *to become young."*
> *Pablo Picasso*

Love

Allowing negativism
to take over
is an insult to myself
and to my Creator.

For I came
into this world
full of potential
for love.

God, help me
to see myself
as you see me,
loving and lovable.

*"If you're not feeling good
 about you,
 what you're wearing outside
 doesn't mean a thing."*
 Leontyne Price

Hope

Every day
seems to be a
challenge:
to give in
or retreat because
the effort is so great—
or to press onward
full of hope,
cherishing
each opening flower,
each new idea,
each valued friend.

Today
I choose to
cherish.

*"The challenge is
to be true
to each stage of life."*
Leo Buscaglia

Newness

All of creation
is a gift.
Whatever burden
I carry with me today,
may I not let it
prevent me from
seeing a world
filled with wonder—
    a newness
        and a freshness
that can revitalilze me
    if I let it.

> *"Stones have been known*
> *to move*
> *and trees to speak."*
>   *William Shakespeare*

Choosing Change

Carrying old guilts around
can be stifling and
destructive,
a real waste of time!

I have within me
the power to change,
to be renewed and
transformed.

At this moment,
I choose to let
God love
life into me.

"I want to unfold.
I don't want to stay
*   folded anywhere,*
because where I am
*   folded*
There I am a lie."
*   Rainer Maria Rilke*

A Sense of Wonder

When I feel small
and insignificant,
  forgotten even,
God, help me not to
turn in upon myself.

Help me to truly
open my eyes,
  as if to see
  people and things
  for the first time.

Fill me again
with wonder.
Re-create the child
  in me.

> *"There is no such thing*
> *as a problem*
> *without a gift for you*
> *in its hands."*
> *Richard Bach*

Contentment

Yes, I'm aging.
I don't deny it,
    hide it,
        or hate it.
I'm retired and I'm glad.
    It's not intolerable.
    It came at a very useful time.

I do what I want
    when I want (usually).
I am not blasted out of bed
    by a rude alarm.
I enjoy family, friends, and hobbies
    when I choose (usually).

I don't need to be popular.
I am content
    to be.

Yes, I'm aging and I like it.

*"Keep your face to the sunshine
and you will not see the
shadows."*
    Helen Keller

Recharging

Mornings are unpredictable.

Once in awhile
I get right in gear.
Usually
it takes some doing.

Today,
nothing in me
wants to move.

Can I listen to my body
and allow myself
a day of rest
without guilt?

Can I say
it's all right to do nothing?

Today, I am going to give myself
permission to recoup,
        regroup,
                and recharge.

"Measure your health by your
sympathy with morning and
Spring."
        Henry David Thoreau

Sharing

This is the time in life
to reflect, to give thanks,
to say
    I was here.
This day
is mine to
make a difference
in the life
    of another.

What do I have
to give?
What can I share?
What have I learned
that will give
hope
    to another?

*"They that plant trees
love others
besides themselves."*
    Thomas Fuller

Searching and Growing

I wonder what I'm capable
of becoming?
And who?
Contrary to what
young people think,
I'm not fully mature.

And I'm glad!

Because if I'm still growing,
then I'm still
searching and
    hoping and
        discerning and
productive!

I am extraordinarily
ordinary.

And I'm alive!

*"We find our individual freedom
by choosing not a destination
but a direction."*
       Marilyn Ferguson

Welcoming Newness

I want to be
as inventive as I can.
As with old cliches, I will
"Take the bull by the horns,"
    "Grab the moment,"
        "Seize the day"!

I will live today
with enthusiasm.
I will keep my eyes open
and welcome new thoughts,
    new ideas,
        new friends.

> *"Boredom*
> *helps one*
> *to make decisions."*
> *Colette*

Beginnings

As I look back
on the springtimes
of my life,
I am amazed
at all the
new beginnings
I have made.

Is it time again
to allow something
to be "newly birthed"
in my life?

> *"Spring...*
> *a natural resurrection,*
> *an experience of*
> *immortality."*
> **Henry David Thoreau**

Accepting Help

I want to be as independent as I can
　　　for as long as possible.
Yet, needing others
has always been a part
of my human experience
　　　even when I wouldn't admit it.

Where is the fine line
between being independent
and accepting help?

Perhaps if I can't yet accept willingly
I can at least be gracious
　　　to those who assist me.

I can be grateful
　　　someone cares.

*"Everything in life that we
really accept
undergoes a change. So
suffering must
become Love. That is the
mystery."*
          Katherine Mansfield

Freedom from Labels

Sometimes
I feel weary of being
put in a slot:
being called
    senior citizen
        old person,
        elderly,
        widowed,
           aged.

I am me.
I am human.
I laugh, I cry,
I sing, I think, I love,
and I can still dance.

God, deliver us
from labels.
Set us free.

*"The compulsion today
is to reduce someone
to what is on the label...
to control...to limit."*
Madeleine L'Engle

The Time—Now

It's time to get out
of my own way.

It's time to finally
do those things
I've intended to do
for so long.

It's time to allow
broken hearts and
hurt feelings to mend,
to heal,
to begin again.

It's time.

> *"There is one thing stronger than all the armies in the world: an idea whose hour is come."*
> Victor Hugo

Savoring Earth

Earth is overflowing
with new life!
Every tulip and lilac
seems ready to burst.

Today
I will savor every
bud about to open,
the crystal clear air,
the bright sun,
and the song of the birds.

I will savor
and be thankful.

> *"Too much of a good thing*
> *can be wonderful."*
> *Mae West*

Oneness

However I have lived
my life up to now—
today I choose to
search for the profound.

I choose to
make connections,
to go down deep within
my soul and
savor my oneness
with my God,
my neighbor,
and the wondrous gifts
of life all around me.

> *"The second half of life*
> *is the spiritual work...."*
> *Carl Jung*

Empathy

Sometimes I wonder
if anyone under
the age of fifty
understands what it's like
        to grow old.

I feel placed
in a category
that often feels
like second class.

I've walked miles and miles
in their shoes.
I wish the
younger generation
would try to walk
one mile
in mine.

*"Personhood
  is not a gift,
  it is an inalienable right."*
  Leo Buscaglia

The Power of Love

If I could just remember
the word "loving"
when I get uptight, pessimistic,
and even bitter,
I'd create a new world for myself
      in a minute.

God, I need an antidote—
a quick antidote—
for those moments
when it all seems to be
      too much.

Teach me how to use
the power of love
to clear my vision
      and renew my spirit.

"Love before
  Love behind
    Love above
    Love below
    Love all around.
    Love will lay
hatred down."
    Navajo prayer

Cherishing New Life

Even if my body
aches today
I can cherish
the wonder of
new life
all about me.

I can sharpen
every working sense,
tune in to all that's new
and watch the person
that I am becoming
stand a little taller.

*"We cannot afford not to fight
for growth and understanding,
even when it is painful,
as it is bound to be."*
May Sarton

Summer

Choices

The newness of spring
evolves into the
blossoming of summer.

Summer offers opportunity
for creating as well as
weeding out.

How can I balance
my time, my energy,
and my awareness?

How much should I
attempt?
What do I leave out?

> *"The greatest thing*
> *in the world is to know*
> *how to be one's own self."*
>   *Michel E. de Montaigne*

Giving My Best

At this empowering time
of my life,
I realize over and over
that the best gift I can give
to those I love
is to be the best me
    that I can be.

If I am striving to be
healthy, happy, and whole,
my efforts invite
loved ones to life,
to enjoyment, and,
most of all,
    to love.

"Old age is like everything else.
To make a success of it,
you've got to start young."
Fred Astaire

The Challenge of Conflict

Adversity and conflict
have their place in life.
If I run from them
    out of fear,
how will I ever know
what my honest thoughts are?

I need the challenge
    to truly determine
        who I am.

Deliver me from bland.

> *"Calamity is the perfect glass*
> *wherein we truly see*
> *and know ourselves."*
> *Sir William D'Avenant*

Gentleness

What has happened
to gentle manners?
Are we in such a hurry
that we can't take time
to treat each other
with dignity?

Today
I will take the time.
Today
I will treat others
as I want to be treated.

> *"True courtesy*
> *is a way of*
> *being in this world*
> *gently,*
> *lovingly,*
> *gracefully."*
> *Author unknown*

Enjoying Retirement

Some of us had to retire,
and some of us wanted to
because we had other things
we were ready to do.

Some of us escaped to see
what "doing nothing"
could be like.
Some of us wanted less pressure
and found we only exchanged pressures.

Some of us dreaded retirement.
Some of us couldn't wait.
Whatever our reasons,
let's enjoy it with imagination!

> *"Absence of occupation is not rest.*
> *A mind quite vacant is a mind*
> *distressed."*
>   *William Cowper*

Others' Needs

Someone needs me
today.

That person
may be close to me
or a stranger.

May I allow myself
to be aware
of how I can be present
to another
who needs to feel
loved.

*"Give what you have.
To someone
it may be better
than you dare to think."*
  Henry Wadsworth Longfellow

Openness

Today
I will stand ready,
arms open wide,
eyes and ears and heart
alert and eager
to receive
the natural wonders
of the beauty around me.

Let me touch
your presence, God,
today.

> *"All creation*
> *teaches us*
> *some way*
> *of prayer."*
>   *Thomas Merton*

Freedom to Be

Freedom to be
is being less concerned
about what people think
of my choices.

I am *me*, and I choose
what I choose.
I am the best judge
of where I am going.

Today I will celebrate
my freedom to
be me.

> *"The strongest principle*
> *of growth*
> *lies in human choice."*
> *George Eliot*

Faith

On foggy mornings
the sun still rises,
whether or not
I see the light.

God,
strengthen my faith
to believe
you are with me
even when I'm
groping to see.

You are light
in my darkness.

> *"Faith is going to the edge*
> *of all we have*
> *and taking one more step."*
> *Author unknown*

Self-Knowledge

It takes practice
to learn what I
really need and want.

It takes even more
practice and a lot of
courage
to make my needs
and wants
known.

God, be with me
as I strive to
figure myself out.

"To ask
for what one wants,
instead of always
waiting for permission."
Virginia Satir

Self-Assessment

In this rich time
of my life,
I want to assess
where I have been
and where I am going.

I ask for
wisdom and light
to see myself as I am,
not afraid of the
dark places
within me,
trusting in a Power
greater than my own.

"Not everything
that is faced can be
changed.
But nothing
can be changed
until it is faced."
James Baldwin

Awareness of Life

What a gift to be alive!

It's so easy to complain—
    but today I won't.

Today I'll keep my eyes wide
and my head high—
open to all the secret
flowers and miracles
that are waiting
for me,
if I
    will
        simply
           look.

> *"Life is not a problem*
> *to be solved, but*
> *a reality to be experienced."*
> *Soren Kierkegaard*

Interests as Gifts

There are so many
people to meet
and places to go
and things to do.

Sometimes I forget that
my interests are gifts.
God, grant me health
to keep my gifts growing.

> *"Learn day by day*
> *to broaden*
> *your horizons."*
> *Ethel Barrymore*

Risking Failure

Fear of failure
can keep me from
living a full life.

How often is
what seems like failure
actually a success.

To be successful,
I must be willing
to risk failure.

> *"Most successes*
> *are built on failures."*
> *Charles Gow*

Trust

Birds in undulating flight
appear to risk
falling after soaring.
Their wings work hard
until they find
a current
to carry them.

Today, I want to allow myself
to be led by God
through the risks
of the dyings and risings
of my day.

> *"If the basis of peace is God,*
> *the secret of peace is trust."*
> *John Benjamin Figis*

Speaking and Listening

It's safe to say
some days
I talk too much.

It's also safe to say
some days I fear
to risk saying anything.

How complex we are!

Today I will depend
on my inner wisdom
to speak or listen,
a wisdom
only experience
can impart.

"Like golden apples in silver settings
are words spoken at the proper time."

Proverbs 25:11 (RSV)

Discarding

Priorities
can make or
shake me.

Today it's time
to root out and discard
those empty *things*
that hold me down
and keep me from soaring.

> *"Some people regard*
> *discipline*
> *as a chore.*
> *For me, it is a*
> *kind of order*
> *that sets me free*
> *to fly."*
> > **Julie Andrews**

Humility

It's amazing how
some people my age
think they finally
know it all and
continually blow
their horns of knowledge.

I pray to be grateful
for all life teaches,
share it willingly
and with love,
mindful always
of how much more
there is to learn.

> *"Without humility*
> *there can be no*
> *humanity."*
> *John Buchan*

Bitterness of Age

The aging process is
taking its toll
in some of my friends.

I grieve to see those
who were once warm-hearted
becoming bitter and critical.

I mourn their unhappiness
and the sad effect it has
on the rest of us.

I long to help and
don't know what to say.

I fear it could happen to me.

> *"The door to the human heart
> can be opened only from the
> inside."*
> **Author unknown**

Knowing Myself

This is the day
I choose to be
more aware
of each present moment.

I will look
with confidence
at my successes
as well as my failures.

I will listen
with hope
to the person
I am today.

> *"To see and hear*
> *what is here,*
> *instead of*
> *what should be,*
> *was, or will be."*
> *Virginia Satir*

Senses

On days when I feel
depleted
I will use every sense
to be filled once again.

I will examine the lines
        on a leaf,
feel the petals
        on a flower,
smell the freshness
        of the earth,
hear the wind
        in a popple tree.

And I will taste
the goodness of the Lord
        all around me.

"*Do you wish to
catch a glimpse
of God?
Look intently
at creation.*"
  Anthony de Mello

The Energy of Creation

Summer
is charged with
color and life!

As the red-gold
rising sun enlivens
every pine and daisy,
every cardinal and chipmunk,
may I too
take strength and courage
from all creation
bursting to life
about me.

"O Great Spirit...
Make me always ready
to come to you
with clean hands
and straight eyes."
              Indian prayer

Searching for the Child

As the noise
of this modern world
tries to fracture me,
I long to
experience life
with deeper discernment.

Perhaps today,
I should visit
with a child
to find a fresh view.

Perhaps today,
I should search for
the child in me.

*"Childhood knows
the human heart."*
Edgar Allen Poe

Becoming Too Serious

Loosen me up, God.
I'm getting too serious,
and that always
gets me in trouble.

If I'm too serious
and structured,
I might miss a great
opportunity
for a new insight.

Give me serendipity!

> *"I find we are growing*
> *serious, and then we are*
> *in great danger*
> *of being dull."*
>> William Congreave

Loving the Questions

At my age
shouldn't I have
more answers?
Why are there still
so many questions?

> Dear Self,
> if you weren't still
> asking questions,
> where would
> your mind be?

> > *"Be patient toward all*
> > *that is unsolved in your heart.*
> > *Try to love the questions*
> > *themselves."*
> > **Rainer Maria Rilke**

Centering

My mind is going
everywhichway
like a swallow in flight
searching for food.
I swoop from
thought to thought,
unable to concentrate
    on one
        for very long.

Center me, Lord.
Don't let me panic
as my brain waves
    change.
Take me down inside
to the peaceful place
    within.
Let me rest
in your care.

"The peaceful are the strong."
Oliver Wendell Holmes

Pain of Memories

Memories can be painful.
But even pain
can be life-giving.

God, help me to
name what happened,
admit it was painful,
and decide how I can
respond differently now.

At this moment,
I choose
to be healed.

> *"Memory
> is the mother
> of all wisdom."*
> *Aeschylus*

Anxiety

Sometimes I forget
that it takes skill
to know where I am.
If I'm sad or anxious,
I'm on the wrong road.
A change in *me*
is needed.

No one
can take away
my peace and joy
unless I let them.

*"Don't let any person
take away your happiness."*
M. Bertha Poupore

Self-Worth

Old oak trees stand
twisted and gnarled—
yet dignified and graceful.

May I stand tall
as possible today,
complete with aches and pains,
confident that
Someone
greater than myself
has created me
and sustains me,
a treasured masterpiece.

> *"You are God's work of art."*
> *St. Paul*

Outward Pressures

The sparrow perched
and gobbled seeds.
The cardinal flew in
and pecked at the sparrow
    to leave.
The sparrow went right on eating.
The cardinal did too.

Today,
I will not allow
outer pressures
to push or crowd me.
I will move and act
from my center
    of peace and poise.

> *"Peace*
> *is seldom denied*
> *to the peaceful."*
>   *J.C.F. Schiller*

Separateness

To my grandchildren,
to the newlyweds
down the block,
or to anyone younger
than me,
I want to say
with the poet,
"I am you,
    grown old."

I also want to say,
"You and I have so much
in common.
Please don't make me
feel separate."

"I am you,
    grown old."

*"If we do not know
what we are going to be,
we cannot know
what we are."*
    Simone de Beauvoir

Self-Sharing

Let me tread gently
today, Lord.
Let me focus my powers
so every thought
    and word,
    every act
    and gesture,
will be life-giving
to those around me,
    then multiply
    and return
as a blessing
    to me and mine.

> *"The marks left*
> *by one individual*
> *on another*
> *are eternal."*
> François Mauriac

The Death of Friends

A very great sadness
of growing older
is losing my friends
through death.

Perhaps this is the day
to write an unsent letter
and express the things
I failed to say
when I had the opportunity.

> *"It is better to have loved
>   and lost
>   than never to have
>   loved at all."*
>   *Alfred Lord Tennyson*

Letting Go

One heartache of parenting
can be watching what your
children choose to do
and allowing them to do it.

May I trust that I
gave them what they needed
when I was
their strongest influence.

May I rest content now
to let them be whoever
they are meant to be,
fortified by my love—
even as my Creator
allows me to be
who I am
and loves me anyway.

*"There are only two lasting
 bequests
 we can give our children,
 one is roots
 the other is wings."*
        Gerry Zachmann

The World's Directions

When the aging process
keeps me from physical activity,
I have time to think more about
where the world is going.

I fear for this modern age
and the wild directions
it seems to take.

But, wisdom says
God has been watching and
allowing human creatures to
be outrageous for eons,
and God cares for us still.

We are who we are.
God help us.

*"When you truly possess all you
have been and done,
which may take some time,
you are fierce with reality."*
   Florida Scott-Maxwell

Age and Happiness

I have a genuine
complaint.

Who gave this society
the notion that
we are happy only
if we're young and
slim and
gorgeous?

If I'm older,
overweight, and
wrinkly,
can't I be happy?

> *"Youth is a gift of nature,*
> *but age is a work of art."*
> *Garson Kanin*

Giving Thanks

As summer's heat
sizzles on,
I give thanks for
air conditioners,
ice-cold drinks,
cotton clothing,
lakes and
     streams and
        rivers and
           oceans,
and I give thanks to
God
who provides
   all this
      for me.

*"The sun does not shine
for a few trees and flowers,
but for the wide world's joy."*
        Harriet Ward Beecher

Forgiveness

Does God weep
over my lack of
fidelity
as I do
over those I love
and nurtured?

God created me
in perfection, yet
I fail
daily.

Strengthen me, God,
to be as forgiving
as I am forgiven
by you.

*"He who cannot
 forgive others
 breaks the bridge
 over which he
 must pass himself."*
       George Herbert

Looking Inward

Busy learning
busy sharing,
busy going from
yesterday to
    today to
        tomorrow.

Does any of it
sink in?
Or do I only
live on the
surface
    of my busyness?

This day
I will slow down,
look inward,
and check my pulse
    for signs
        of *inner* life.

"To really know...is to be
transformed by what one knows."
Anthony de Mello

Loneliness

The lonely of this world
are crying out for love.
Sometimes I am one who cries out,
and sometimes I am one
who is able to take
the hand of another
    who is crying.

How very much
we need each other.
How very much we need
to be heard
and valued
and accepted
    just as we are.

And how life-giving it is
to listen, to appreciate,
to welcome
    another.

> *"We need to have people who
> mean something to us—people
> to whom we turn knowing that
> being with them is coming home."*
> *Bernard Cooke*

Age and Attitude

We have all been aging
since the day we were born.

Who decided
that at a certain age
we are suddenly
"over the hill"?

I am only as old as I feel
and I feel "on top of the hill."
I can look back and
appreciate the climb
and I look forward with trust
to the rest of the journey.

> *"Age is a matter of mind,*
> *if you don't mind*
> *it doesn't matter."*
> **Author unknown**

Peace of Heart

It's tempting to think
I can do nothing
about the turmoil
    in the world.

But I can.

I can make my heart
a center of peace,
then allow this peace
to radiate out
to every person
    I meet today.

> *"A person of hope*
> *says we are*
> *shapers of history."*
>   *Dr. Helen Caldicott*

Choosing Attitudes

I have a choice
in how I think.
The attitudes I hold
are up to me,
not dependent on
what may or may not
happen to me.

Today
I choose to let go of
stress and strain.
Today
I work with God
and will accomplish
all I need to do.

"...it is how we perceive ourselves and how these thought processes affect our behavior that determines our successes or failure in life."

        John and Helen Boyle

Renewing Quality of Life

In these fading days
of summer,
each hour of light
becomes more valuable.

While parts of me
are winding down,
I sense a challenge
to renew
my quality of life.

I have within me
the power to decide
whether I shall
grow old artfully
or just grow old.

*"...everything can be
taken from a person but
one thing:...the freedom
to choose one's attitudes."*
Viktor Frankl

Wholeness of Life

Some days
it's easier to feel
sorry for myself
than to count my blessings.
Today, at least
I see that life
is gift,
part of a great whole.

I am a child
of the Universe.
Truly blessed.

*"Just to be
is a blessing;
just to live
is holy."*
    Abraham Heschel

Index

About the author

Pat Corrick Hinton grew up in southwest Minneapolis. She became an elementary school teacher, with a degree in English and Education from the College of St. Catherine in St. Paul, and taught in private and public schools in the Twin Cities area for fourteen years.

In 1965 she married Jim Hinton. After their daughter, Laura, was born—followed a year later by their son, Mark—Pat began a writing career at home. As the children grew, Pat's writing centered mostly around the concerns of a young family.

Her first book, *Prayer after Nine Rainy Days*, geared toward families and children, was published in 1978 and became a best seller. During her children's junior high school years, she wrote two more books—*Prayers for Growing and Other Pains*, published in 1981, and *Images of Peace, Reflections on Everyday Peacemaking*, in 1984. All three books were published by Winston Press.

Her other writing includes curriculum texts and fiction, as well as articles and poems for a variety of magazines.

Pat has been working with senior citizens for the past seven years as instructor in journal-keeping and life-storytelling at the Richfield Community Center near Minneapolis.